Self-Compassion

- I Don't Have To Feel Better Than Others To Feel Good About Myself

Learn How To See Self Esteem Through The Lens Of Self-Love and Mindfulness and Cultivate The Courage To Be You

Table Of Contents

Introduction

The world is a vast, complicated and sometimes downright hostile place. Today, more than ever, human beings have had to learn new ways to be resilient, know themselves and have the courage to be who they are. Our hyper connected world bombards us with images of phenomenally successful celebrities together with the expectation that we should want nothing but the best for ourselves at all times. But in a bustling world of 7 billion people, carving out a meaningful niche for ourselves can be daunting to say the least.

It's understandable that people feel the need to bolster their self esteem. Faced with millions of glossy images in the media about how we should live our lives, some have turned to trying even harder still to keep up. Others have merely given up. It's no exaggeration that people in the 21st century live in a world of infinitely more possibilities than any generation before them. We have experts and gurus of all stripes telling us that the life we have now is nothing compared to what we could achieve – and yet, we're as depressed and lacking in confidence as ever.

Self help books on the market today will tell you one of two things: either that you are perfect already as you are and needn't worry, or that with just a little (well, a lot) of effort, you *can* reach those goals. Be the best, smartest, most successful, thinnest and relentlessly happiest version of yourself possible. No excuses!

This book takes a different approach to self esteem altogether. If you're feeling overwhelmed and worthless, inundated with information, struggling to juggle life, expectations, and disappointments... it may be time for a little self-compassion.

Unlike self esteem or an inflated confidence level, self-compassion is a different way of looking at yourself and others, warts and all, and a way more realistic acceptance of the way things are. With self-compassion, you become unflappable, calm and self-assured - without the risk of narcissism or becoming self-absorbed. Through a series of exercises, this book will suggest a new, gentle yet extremely powerful attitude shift that can end feelings of self-hatred, doubt, shame and low self-worth forever.

Chapter One: What is Self-Compassion?

You may be familiar with the idea of compassion for *others*. When we have compassion for another person, we acknowledge that they are suffering, and feel kindness and good will towards them. Rather than pity, self-compassion is about non-judgmentally accepting others for who they are in the here and now. Rather than judging them for their shortcomings, weaknesses or failures, compassion is about care, kindness and respect.

Self-compassion is turning this kindness to ourselves. It's ironic that many times, people who treat others with acceptance and tenderness can't seem to summon up those same feelings for themselves. While they may be quick to forgive the transgressions of others, they berate themselves harshly for making those very same mistakes.

Self-compassion means we honor and acknowledge our humanity, our imperfection and our fragility. Self-compassion allows you to open your heart up to human condition – and no matter who we are, we all experience a shared humanity. Rather than wanting to change because we find ourselves unacceptable, we change because we *want* to, and because we can look at our shortcomings honestly and without ego.

When we are self-compassionate, we don't have to "do" anything. We can simply allow ourselves to be. Waking up to our own innate value as human beings has profound effects on the way we feel about ourselves, others and the world we live in. Self-compassion permeates all areas of our lives - the physical, emotional, psychological and spiritual. Our interactions with strangers as well as those we love will change subtly, leaving us kinder and more at peace.

Self-acceptance of our bodies

Self-compassion means observing your body with acceptance. Our culture has an almost psychotic preoccupation with youth and beauty, but when we have compassion for our bodies, we neither love nor hate them, we only see and accept them for what they are. At any one time, people may feel that sure, they'll love themselves, just as soon as they lose a little weight or fix their hair or get rid of that zit.

Instead, try to become curious about your body. Get to know it like you would an interesting new friend. What does it like? What can it do? In what ways is it completely unlike every other body? In what ways is it completely unremarkable?

Self-acceptance of our emotions

In our self-help culture, we preach self-love from the mountaintops – except of course, if your self happens to be depressed, belligerent, strange or anxious. In fact, the entire human experience is chopped into halves: positive emotions and negative emotions – the latter being an eternal source of consternation. Negative emotions are only tolerated as incomplete stages on the path to perfection, an assumed future where you will not struggle, will not be unsure and will not, under any circumstances, be unhappy.

But what happens to your unhappiness when you are happy to have it?

Let go of a one-sided view of what it's like to be human. Fully embrace your emotions – the pleasant as well as the not so pleasant. Be OK with the fact that sometimes, you will be unhappy. Those feelings will pass. In fact, *all* feeling will pass.

Self-acceptance of our thoughts

Closely tied to our emotions, our thoughts are also part of us. You can choose to completely identify with a thought, you can choose to deny it, or you can take a step back and merely observe it. Self-compassion means becoming comfortable with your internal landscape for what it is.

When we have self-compassion, we develop a deep, internal resilience that is unshakeable. Whether it's a hurtful comment from someone else or failing at something important to us, self-compassion allows us to look at the events of our lives with kindness. When we do so, we don't beat ourselves up when we fail to reach our goals, nor do we need to boast and brag to feel better about our achievements. The self-compassionate person doesn't look to others for validation. Instead, they seem to generate their own self-worth, enjoying being who they are, filled with the courage to face life without needing to be perfect.

The Science of Self-compassion

Self-compassion is not just something that *sounds* good – more and more, research is being done to show that practicing compassion has real, measurable effects on our health, our work, our relationships and our lives in general.

Research has shown that when we blame others for our mistakes, we tend to feel less compassionate towards them[i]; that when we have compassion for others our own happiness increases[ii]; that compassion makes us better parents[iii]; that it lowers stress hormones in the body and boosts the immune system[iv]; makes us better friends[v] and can even reduce the risk of heart disease[vi]. Self-compassion floods the body with feel-good neurotransmitters, improves our sleep and reduces stress levels. For anyone who knows how closely the mind and body are connected, this should come as no surprise.

Chapter Two: Self-compassion and Self Esteem

For anyone raised in the modern Western world, "self-compassion" might sound suspiciously like regular old garden variety "self esteem". It's the reason your kindergarten teacher put "Great Job!" stickers on your crayon drawings and why group meeting leaders are told to encourage everyone to add something positive to their criticisms. It's curious that just a few generations after the bootstrap idealism of the American Dream is over, we are left with the fuzzy democracy of the idea that everyone deserves to be special. Or rather, that everyone deserves to try and be as special as they can.

Self-compassion and self esteem are two vastly different concepts, and proponents of the confidence-for-everyone-all-the-time model have begun to see that there are limits to what at first seemed like an obviously good idea. What could be so bad about feeling good about yourself?

Well, one of the main problems with self esteem is that it's fragile. Built on external evaluation, self esteem can be instantly undermined by someone who simply does better than you. A mother who constantly gives her child affection when they perform well at school is not giving that child the message that they are intrinsically valuable as a human being.

Rather, the message is that affection, achievement, recognition and feelings of self-worth are all tied to measurable external phenomenon. This means they can be taken away. That child may be said to have a high self esteem, but what will happen when they encounter a peer who does better than them at school?

Self-compassion, on the other hand, is not about measurable quantities, and there are no conditions attached to it. We should have compassion for ourselves and others because life is hard, and we are all doing the best we can. We don't have to do anything to earn self-compassion, we can enjoy it merely by virtue of being human, of living the best way we know how, of being the only thing we can be: what we are.

Creating high self esteem seems like a reasonable goal on its face, but it has a built in trap that is designed to leave us unhappier, less accomplished, less kind. What's worse, when we are constantly incentivized by praise and recognition for doing well, we eventually stop trying to do well *for its own sake*. Tying up our self-concept with external measures damages us – but it also saps the joy from doing something well, from the enjoyment of genuine achievement. It makes us believe, perhaps unwittingly, that things that others don't acknowledge as valuable actually aren't, and that good actions that aren't recognized as such don't really count.

The idealism of a high self esteem also means that being average is nowhere good enough. The irony is that we all strive to be exceptional, to be better than everyone else, but, merely by looking at the statistical reality, most of us will not be.

Let that sink in for a moment.

How does it feel, to be in the middle? To be good enough, to be fine, to be regular and average? If you've ingested any self-help material from the better portion of this century, this thought alone is probably enough to have you kicking and screaming internally. In fact, when you hear the word "average" you probably just round down to "failure". This is the reason why psychometrists who test young children are trained not to say "your child has an average score on the IQ test" but rather, "your child is scoring in the same range as his peers". For a parent, you see, being "average" is more or less the same thing as having a problem. It's far more comforting to hear the result framed as at least keeping up with everybody else.

What is on the other side of the desperate desire to be unique? What seems aspirational quickly dissolves into self-absorption, shallowness, insecurity, and vanity.

Psychologists and mental health professionals have long

understood that the root of narcissism is shame. To the outsider, the narcissist simply looks like he has far too much self esteem and could probably stand to be taken down a notch. But look deeper into the mind of a narcissist and you will see that an over inflated ego very often forms in response to damage done to that ego. In other words, low self esteem and high self esteem are two sides of the same coin. Perhaps you know somebody like this. After being rejected by a particular group, they claim they never cared for the group anyway – in other words, that it is *them* who is doing the rejecting.

Self-compassion is not binary in the same way that self esteem is. To put it very simply, you needn't be better than someone else to be good. Self esteem is relativistic, competitive and zero sum. There can only be one winner, and you increase your chances of that being you by putting down anyone who threatens to take that place. It's you or them. Dog eat dog. This competition is built into our very language. Good, better, best. There is a continuum and we belong somewhere on it. When we say "better", it is implied that we mean "better than X". When our self-concept is this easy to damage, it makes sense that we are serious about defending it.

Self-compassion, on the other hand, is not about beating opponents, or even beating yourself. There is no comparison -

you are kind and good to yourself simply because. Rather than look at your life, your body, your skills and your accomplishments and see only what could be improved, what is not as good as everyone else's, what is better than everyone else's, you look and see simply what is. You accept what is because... well, it is.

When we are self-compassionate we understand that realistically, most of the time we will land somewhere in the big, meaty middle of the bell curve. We understand that we can make plans, but sometimes we will fail. Sometimes we will fall short of perfection (in fact, we basically always fall short of perfection). So, instead of looking at our lives with a built in scorecard, we simply see what we see.

The joy of high self esteem tied to an external event feels great, but there's always hidden inside it a little seed of anxiety, of paranoia that recognizes that it is not permanent. Self-compassion, on the other hand, is nothing more or less than the full acknowledgement and acceptance of whatever it is that you are. It cannot be threatened.

Sure, you think, but isn't it a little dangerous to just accept everything? Isn't that the same as being passive, as completely giving up? What goals could you have if you don't strive for anything?

Sadly, most of us can't even imagine what it would look like to be motivated by anything other than shame and fear. Since we were children, we've been taught that there are only two opposite things: achievement, and failure. We are trained in school to move away from the embarrassment and disappointment of a "failure" and towards the glory and satisfaction of winning and achievement. The good guys beat the bad guys in all the movies.

But again, this is very simple, dualistic thinking. In fact, when we really accept and look at who we are - not what we wish we were or what we think we should be - we see ourselves more clearly than ever. Without either shame or excessive pride, we can see our faults clearly for what they are. Many people fail to grasp the meaning of "acceptance" simply because they have never actually experienced it themselves. It does not mean you condone what you look at. It also doesn't mean you condemn it. Instead, acceptance is neutral, obvious. What would happen if you looked at yourself the same way as you look at a blue sky? If you accepted all the things you were the same way you accepted the fact that the sky is blue?

The project of self esteem is not to realize who you are and feel good about it. The rule of self esteem is that you can only feel good about yourself as soon as you meet some goal or standard. When you have a goal, everything that doesn't affirm or lead to that goal is dismissed or ignored. This leads to denial or trivializing of the parts of your being that could actually use improvement. If looking honestly at your flaws is a painful and embarrassing process, one that only makes you feel more worthless, you're less inclined to ever really look at those flaws. And less inclined to fix them.

With self-compassion, you can look at yourself objectively and make realistic moves to learn more skills and improve on your weaknesses. Self-compassion doesn't mean shrugging our shoulders at our flaws, but rather taking a good, honest look at them and seeing them for what they are. Without judgment. When we let go of the constant need to fix ourselves up, to be better, the paradox is that we open our eyes to becoming better anyway.

Self Esteem	Self-compassion
Relative – you feel good *compared* to someone else feeling bad	Absolute – you feel good, end of story
All about competition. Feeling valuable only when ranked against others (or even an older version of	All about common humanity. Your value is neither undermined or enhanced by the value of others

yourself)	
Conditional	Unconditional
Based on striving, which is moving away from the present reality and towards a goal	Based on acceptance, which moves towards the present moment
Quantifiable	Non-quantifiable
Reduces our empathy for others – compassion is "zero sum"	Enhances our empathy and compassion for others
Is elite and exclusive, only exceptionalism and uniqueness is valuable	Is inclusive, all humans deserve to feel self-compassion
Too much can lead to narcissism, vanity and self-absorption	The concept of "too much self-compassion" is meaningless
Self-improvement comes from external sources, from fear and shame	Self improvement is internal, proactive and aspirational
Flaws are not part of the picture, so are ignored or denied	Flaws are part of reality and accepted
Idealistic	Realistic

Chapter Three: Self-compassion Exercises

What follows are some tools you may find useful in opening yourself up to more self-compassion in your life. These are only suggestions though, and you should feel free to be inspired to change these exercises to suit your own unique situation. If something resonates with you, see if you can use those ideas in the way you think of yourself day to day. If not, shelve the exercise and go back instead to the ones that really speak to you. The goal is shifting your mindset away from thinking rooted in relativistic, competitive self esteem and into a truly accepting and compassionate frame of mind – exactly how you do this is unimportant.

Exercise One: "There I Go"

There is a lot of wisdom in the truism, "the world is your mirror". The way we feel about others, about life in general, is often a reflection of how we feel about ourselves. The most important relationship you can have is with yourself, so it's no surprise that the quality of that relationship would be echoed in all of your interactions with others. It's for this reason that the following exercise can be so effective.

This exercise is a self-compassion exercise that focuses on others. We'll start with this paradoxical exercise for two reasons. Firstly, empathy and understanding for others, and empathy and understanding for ourselves, are closely linked. Strengthening our capacity for one inevitably strengthens the ability for the other. The second reason, though, is that it is often easier to have compassion for others than it is for ourselves. For a host of reasons, people seem to find it easier to look clearly at the lives of others than their own – starting with compassion for others is a good way of obliquely beginning to develop compassion for yourself.

The exercise:

Choose any day or moment to begin. You don't need to wait for an appropriate moment to start, just start now. The moment is right. As you move around your day, turn your attention outwards to the people you encounter. This includes the people you work with and family members, but also people you pass in the street for a few seconds, waiters and waitresses, people on the TV... anyone really.

As you pass them, instead of letting your self say things like "there goes that guy, look at him, walking with his dog, wearing those pants..." change the pronouns and substitute yourself, saying "there *I* go, look at *me*, walking *my* dog, wearing *my* pants". And so on.

This might feel bizarre at first. Keep it up though. Simply change your original thoughts and perceptions about other people to be about yourself.

"Look at me, screaming and having a temper tantrum in the supermarket."
"There I go, looking pretty hot to be honest."
"There I am, probably 80 years old. I feel so tired. I need a cane to walk."

Have fun with it and try it out on different people. People you like and dislike, people you are indifferent towards. People who are very, very different from you and also those you identify with. Turn all your thoughts about them, good and bad, towards yourself.

After a while of doing this, you might start to notice something strange happening. The kid screaming in the supermarket, the one who would usually elicit pure irritation from you, suddenly becomes something more familiar, especially when you invite your brain to remember, *you were once a child, too.* You probably once had a tantrum in a supermarket yourself. Maybe, you even did something more irritating as a child. Suggest this to your mind, and you open yourself to the thought that, in a way you *are* that child in the supermarket. You sometimes lose your temper, you're sometimes insufferable and sulky when you don't get what you want, aren't you? When you think about it, you have a lot in common with that child.

Human beings love to separate themselves into groups, "me" and "not me", but when you play around with these barriers, you might begin to feel that they are a lot more flexible than they at first seem. No matter who it is, you can inevitably find a way to identify with them, with their experience.

And it goes even deeper. Once you start looking at people not as separate, alien, unknowable beings far outside of you, but as people who share in the human experience, the same experience that you do, you may feel a deeper, almost inexplicable sense of connection and fellowship with them. As all of us move about our lives, we all experience difficulties and joys, we all feel the highs and lows of the human drama, we all worry about death, we all celebrate love, we all die, we all love.

This exercise can remind you that in the bigger picture, there is no competition. We are all human. If you can cultivate an amazed curiosity about others, an appreciation for everything they are, every little variation on the rich tapestry of existence, it will be that much easier to turn that lens on yourself. You are not a failure, you are not too fat or too old or too stupid. You are something much more than that: you are part of the immense human condition, and your struggles are not small, private failings – they're nothing less than part of what it means to be alive.

Exercise Two: Authentically You

Think of a famous person you know or admire (well, you don't even need to admire them, any celebrity will do). Think of all the things that make up who they are. How do people instantly recognize who this celebrity is? It could be a prominent feature, a distinct style of talking or dress, an outlandish world-view or a history of doing very particular things. Now, imagine them *without* this trait. Make Larry King sit up straight and look 10 years younger, make Marilyn Monroe a brunette or give Mick Jagger a beer belly and a conservative dress sense.

Instantly, they lose their authenticity. You could "improve" on any celebrity in this way. Make them skinnier, better looking or smarter. And they *would be* skinnier, better looking and smarter. But they wouldn't be themselves anymore, either. The thing that makes them stand out, the thing that people know and love about them, would be gone.

We have a very simplistic way of thinking of self-worth, of the value of human beings. When we position people on a continuum where one end is bad and the other end is good, we wash out all the subtle variations and idiosyncrasies that make people who they are. We are all blessed with a unique and interesting blend of characteristics, one that is truly ours and nobody else's, and yet we behave as if our being is merely a performance, one that can be quantified, measured and evaluated. Albert Einstein was famously bad at High School Maths (I don't know if this is really true, but it doesn't matter). This fact doesn't detract from his position as one of mankind's most influential thinkers, it *adds* to it.

But there is no box on your standard High School report card that the teacher can tick if she wants to express that young Albert is a restless, brilliant, and dangerously out-of-the-box thinker. She can only give him a percentage value, a letter-grade, and rank him according to his peers on how he performed on a pen and pencil test. What was the essence of Albert Einstein – the lateral thinker, the budding genius who rewrote long-held scientific tenets, the icon with the crazy hair – all of that disappears instantly.

The Exercise

Assume you are famous. Assume, also, that you are famous

exactly as you are now, sitting right here and reading this in this very moment. What are *your* prominent, memorable features? What are the things that make you who you are, "good" or "bad"? How would people instantly recognize you?

Have you got something unusual or noteworthy about your appearance? What do people usually notice about you first? What is the one way you differ from your family and group of friends? Perhaps you have a unique history, a strange way of talking, a wild personal philosophy, an unusual collection of skills, a mole shaped like a dog's head on your left butt cheek, a temper you believe you inherited from your mother, a big, ugly nose, an extra chromosome, a secret, a cat who's like your child, a job you're passionate about, the ability to eat very hot things... whatever.

Don't be tempted to only think of the odd, the unusual or the brag-worthy, though. That is just the old mechanism of "self esteem" coming through. Also think of all the ways you, to put it bluntly, suck. Maybe you never learnt to ride a bike despite trying millions of times. Maybe you have a difficult mental illness, a history with bad relationships or shocking dress sense. Think of the things you've failed at, your personal shortcomings, your mistakes, and the things that make you intensely, utterly annoying to certain people. Remember, many celebrities are famous for these "bad" things as much as anything else.

Now, sit with these things. The good and the bad. The underwhelming. Look at these things and be grateful for them as the things that make you who you are. Resist the urge to rush in and fix up. Resist the urge to deny or cover up or make things sound better than they really are. Resist the urge to judge and quantify.

If you can manage, pick one thing on the list and even *amplify* it. Just to see what happens. Really enjoy this single characteristic that is yours and only yours. Explore it to the fullest. Don't force yourself to be bubbly when you've always been quiet and a bit brooding. If you have crazy, uncontrollable hair, grow it even longer and draw attention to it, letting it be as crazy as it wants. Dress to emphasize your "figure flaws", confess to your boss that you don't know what they're talking about and if someone asks you how you spent your weekend, tell them in all honesty that you sat around in your pajamas, and loved it.

Authentic people, those who are not only comfortable and at home in their own personal reality, but who *thrive* there, these are people who are immune to the precariousness of a "high self esteem" and indifferent to other people's opinions of them. When the only yardstick you have is yourself, you are suddenly not competing with anyone else. Practice *not* ranking yourself. Merely feel what it feels like to be who you are, in all your wonderful, imperfect glory.

Exercise Three: Gratitude Journal

Perhaps "self-compassion" sounds a little soft – as if we should only have "compassion" (i.e. pity) for all the ways we fall far from the ideal. But self-compassion is not a consolation prize for not being more amazing. It's not a resignation to our flaws or merely tolerating them. Instead, self-compassion is very much about taking joy in who we are – *all* of who we are.

One of the best paths to joy is gratitude. You may have discovered this for yourself: that those who are happiest seldom have that much more than you, or know anything special that you don't yet know. Rather, they are able to access and really appreciate the sources of joy they already have in their lives.

This exercise takes you out of the standard "self-help" narrative and asks you not to build up your self esteem, not to increase competition, pursuit and achievement in your life, but to come awake to what is already perfect in your life, right now.

The Exercise

Your Journal needn't be an actual book, but this is a good way to start. You can choose the details. The idea is to have a safe place to store your memories and feelings of joy, delight, bliss. We all have moments of transcendence in our lives, whether we find it in the eyes of our children, in a beautiful landscape, in our bodies, in the pleasure of dancing, being in nature or having a good belly laugh at the ridiculousness of life.

A gratitude journal is not about making goals or fixing yourself up, it's about being grateful for all the miracles in your life you may already be numb to, right now. When we are receptive to the beauty and wonder in life, we may start to notice that we find more of it. In strange places, even.

Things you could include in your journal:

- Memories of the happiest moments you can remember in your life – really enjoy getting into the details of who, when, why. Use all your senses when bringing them back to life.

- Pictures that capture certain emotions of bliss or joy for you – these can be artful pictures of natural beauty or silly photos of cats, it doesn't matter. It only matters that you choose images that stir something positive in you.

- Just like your mother may have asked you to do, make a list of all the things you are grateful to have in your life. Read over this list when life starts to feel a little barren or hostile. You may have forgotten how lucky you are in many, many ways.

- Put in mementos or trinkets from happy events – movie ticket stubs, photos of your loved ones, an heirloom recipe from your grandmother that whisks you back to your childhood, pressed flowers, quotes or poems that moved you, articles, jokes, even compliments you have received in the past that made you glow at the time.

Our modern fix-up culture treats the intricacies of each person's unique life as something that constantly needs a little lifestyle DIY, constantly requiring reworking and streamlining. We are told to value lists of "hacks" that help you shave off seconds of your routine so you can be just that little bit more productive, how to cram more vitamins and "super-foods" into your diet (not like, you know, the regular boring food that losers eat!), how to exercise at your desk to save time, how to always be better, better, better.

It's exhausting. And it rests on one fundamental premise: you are not good enough as you are. Life is not good enough as it is. Your daily routine? Terrible. Your diet? Shocking and shameful. Do you have a life purpose? A tribe? Do you even meditate?!

Cut this kind of thing off at the root: tune in to all the ways your life isn't, in fact, a complete and utter failure. Refuse to be mobilized and energized by shame and dissatisfaction. When you continually look at your life – your wonderful, unique, miraculous life – and wish it was something else, you are ironically cutting yourself off from the one source of joy that actually is available to you.

Exercise Four: Peace and Letting Go of Being Reactive

As long as you base your behavior on what happens around you, your behavior is not truly your own. In a reactive frame of mind, we are like a balloon getting blown around in the wind, going along with whatever breeze is strongest, liable to pop by accident, without direction or intention.

People who live reactive lives are forever caught up in the turmoil of this and that, people's opinions, fashions, habit – millions of little breezes forever pushing them in different directions. When a reactive person is pushed, they respond accordingly. They don't respond because responding is a good thing in that moment or because they want to respond. They just do it, without thinking.

When a reactive person is complimented, their mental balloon goes along with that breeze: they are happy, suddenly their self-worth is higher. But, by the same token, when someone insults them, their mental balloon bobs back in the other direction. Now, they are worthless. You could spend your whole life in this back and forth.

"Letting go" sounds like becoming loose and unconcerned, like the balloon, but the paradox is that when we can really let go of external sources of judgment and appraisal, we tap into our own personal gravity, we become more solid, less likely to be blown every which way by the breezes around us. A person who is not reactive but *active* is aware of and acknowledges both compliments and insults, but doesn't change their beliefs about their self-worth in response to either.

The Exercise:

Work on your non-reactivity. If you have done any of the previous exercises, you may have started to develop a sense of your own self-worth – *a self-worth that does not depend in the slightest on others' opinion of you.* You'll know self-compassion when you feel it. It's unshakeable. As a worthwhile human being, a being living as only you know how, there is a dignity and unflappability to everything you do. This is *your* life. What could someone possible say to undermine the value in that? Similarly, what is the value, really, in being awesome if that awesomeness rests only on whether someone else thinks so at one particular moment?

Nurture the core inside of you, that core that is beyond relative value, beyond public opinion. Let nothing disturb it. Many self esteem books on the market today want as their end goal for you to believe that you're absolutely beautiful, wonderful and uniquely amazing. A creature of unparalleled genius, rarity and excellence. You may be, of course, but chances are, you aren't. Watch out for this message – hidden in what looks like "positive thinking" is in fact the assumption that your goal should always be perfection, should always be high self esteem. That is, you need to be a winner.

Instead, nurture something better than that. Choose to be resilient enough to not need a constantly inflated sense of ego to function properly in the world. Believe, deeply, that you are neither super-fabulous nor completely worthless, but something more than both: a human being, with a life that has value, whatever the circumstances. Whatever happens, that core remains. Become a heroin addict and land up in jail? That core remains the same. Become a multi-billionaire developing a cancer cure and find the love of your life while on a humanitarian mission in the Third World? The core is the same.

Let other people's comments of you wash right off. Their opinions belong to them, not you. Don't bring it into your self-concept.

The other side of this exercise is to treat others the same way. Notice when you assign value to other people, to their actions, to their experience. Is it your right to evaluate them? Watch out for judgmental attitudes seeping into your dealings with others, even the "benign" kind of judgment:

- "I hate going to that club, the music is crap and it's full of posers" (Are you sure? What gives you specifically the ability to say what music is good or bad, or assign value to the way people dress or behave?)

- "He's just had his 50th birthday, and he *still* manages to complete a marathon every year. Age is just a number!" (If it were, it wouldn't seem so incredible to mention it. Are you maybe assuming that being older is intrinsically less valuable, and if someone appears to be doing something valuable while old, this is something that deserves a remark?)

- "You're so brave! I could never be that fearless." (From

another perspective, bravery is foolhardiness. Depending on the context, caution may be more valuable. When you compare yourself to others, even favorably, even to give them a compliment, you are doing you both a disservice)

Make an effort to let value judgments pass over you instead of taking them as gospel. In ordinary life, throw-away comments like the above barely register and if you were to start dissecting them you'd likely end up with nothing to say about anything. But meaningless comments have a way of seeping deeper down into our consciousness, making themselves a part of how we actually think of ourselves. In other words, say it often enough and it becomes true. Don't accept people's judgment of you and refrain from judging others.

Chapter Four: The Roller Coaster of Self Esteem

Here are some signs that you seek external validation, in other words, that your self-concept is like the balloon in the wind. See if any of these sound like they describe you, and think carefully of anything that isn't on this list, too.

- You often feel like your entire mood can be spoiled with just one mean comment.

- You have several people in your life that you enjoy feeling superior to.

- You sometimes tally up your achievements in a list to determine how you compare against others in life.

- You have occasionally done something only because you knew it would get a good response.

- You frequently pass judgment on the choices, appearance or value of people around you.

- You bear grudges against others.

- Alternatively, you feel deeply damaged or broken somehow,

maybe even completely unlovable.

- You feel very much worse or better than other people.

- You think that other people get to decide whether someone is good or not.

- You're a perfectionist.

- You sometimes have difficulties making decisions, or accepting the one you do finally make.

- You absolutely *hate* to receive negative feedback or criticism.

- You worry a lot about how you come across to other people.

- You exaggerate about how awful or how wonderful you are, even resorting to lying outright.

- You tend to blame other people for the bad things that happen in your life.

- You make excuses, i.e. there always seems to be something getting in your way.

- You depend a lot on others to take care of you.

- You sometimes feel like cutting everyone out of your life.

- You take things in life very seriously and have trouble laughing things off.

- You self deprecate in public or else put other people down.

- You don't like the idea of change.

- You feel like a lot of your identity is in the things you own.

- You're very concerned with what others think of you, and you spend a lot of time trying to guess what exactly other people are thinking about you.

Now, you may have noticed that the above list contains "symptoms" of both high and low self esteem. This may seem strange if you've been led to believe that these things are opposites of each other. Actually, both high and low self esteem are states of mind that result from basing our sense of self-worth on external events. When those events tell us we are worthwhile, we are said to have high self esteem, and when they tell us we're bad, we have low self esteem. But the underlying mechanism is largely the same: we are adjusting our moods, our actions and our beliefs in our worth as human beings on things that are outside ourselves.

All goes well so long as what's outside us affirms and praises who we are – nobody is immune to feeling special simply because someone has complimented them. But we can really get a sense of how tenuous this good feeling is when that same person insults us or withdraws their praise. It's for this reason that the goal should not be increasing one's self esteem, but rather dismantling the belief that our sense of self-worth is something that other people give us or something we take or earn by doing good. Healthier than a high self esteem is a realistic, compassionate view of ourselves – and others. Generating our sense of self-worth from within means we have a more stable self-concept – one that can endure criticism while still learning from it. One that can honestly appraise who we are as human beings – and love and respect ourselves anyway.

Wabi-Sabi – an Aesthetic of Imperfection

There is an ancient Japanese art called Kintsugi, where the chips and cracks in crockery are repaired with fine gold. Rather than throwing something that is damaged away, or even trying to invisibly repair it so that it seems like it never broke at all, a cup or vase treated with Kintsugi is honored for the broken and imperfect thing it is. The philosophy behind this is very touching. What is damaged is merely part of the reality for the life of the item, even enhancing its value. Highlighting the seams and imperfections, we accept that breakage, wear and tear are all part of life – and that they can even be beautiful.

The Japanese have a term for this kind of aesthetic – Wabi Sabi. At the root of the philosophy behind Wabi Sabi are three principles: nothing lasts, nothing is perfect and nothing is finished. Items that show this flawed beauty, that highlight the limitations of life, are embraced and not labeled deficient. In pottery, deliberate chips or asymmetries in artifacts are seen as a reminder of the impermanence in life. The wistfulness and yearning we experience on perceiving these imperfections is understood to be an important precursor to enlightenment.

Here's the paradox: when we strive for permanence, when we tolerate only perfection and when we assume that one day our work doing both of these things will be finished and we can finally relax, we are setting ourselves up for disappointment. However, embracing the fact that everything in life, our life included, is a little wonky, a work in process and something that occasionally breaks, will lead us to a more profound sense of permanence, perfection and completeness.

Perhaps we could all learn something from the Japanese in

this regard. Rather than struggling to cover up our flaws, to hide our damage or deny our imperfections, we can simply accept and even embrace them. That we can be loved, valuable and worthwhile not in spite of our flaws, but even *because* of them is something we are not often taught to do as children, or encouraged to do as adults.

Nothing lasts:

What happens when you accept and embrace the impermanence around you? Our best qualities will one day disappear with the passing of time, as will our worst. The struggles we are having now are not forever, nor are the pleasures. What remains?

Nothing is perfect:

Can you accept that there is, at least not on this earth, nothing completely faultless? Instead of mourning the impossibility of something perfect, can you love what is?

Nothing is finished:

As we attain one goal, the next goal immediately becomes apparent. Can you let go of the need to have closure, and just let life unfold as it will?

Chapter Five: Putting Self-compassion Into Action

Daily Self-compassion: It's the Little Things

What follows are some statements and thoughts, each of them framed differently. The first two demonstrate thinking from a more traditional, self esteem framework. One shows an absence of self esteem and the other the presence of it, but both of them still place the locus of control externally instead of internally, and so both are more or less variations of one another. The third sentence shows an alternative stemming from a position of self-compassion.

<u>First scenario:</u>

1. "I have to lose weight to look sexy."
2. "Real men love curves. My husband adores mine."

Self-compassion: "I think that model is so beautiful. But I don't want her body – mine's fine as it is."

While the first gives power to men in general, the second gives power to just one specific man. Although the second person might be perceived as having higher self esteem, there is no real difference in the quality of the self-concept in both. The third statement doesn't argue or compete, merely asserts that the person has self-worth anyway – and that the only person who matters in this issue is themselves. Also note that the person in the third statement doesn't need to put down a beautiful model in order for them to love their own body.

<u>Second scenario:</u>

1. "Life is meaningless. I want to just crawl into a hole and die."
2. "Don't say that! That's such a negative way of thinking!"

Self-compassion: "Man, I'm in a bad mood today. I'm just going to veg out in front of the TV till it passes."

The first statement expresses dissatisfaction that life is a particular way, but the second sentence is no better in that it expresses dissatisfaction with particular ways of thinking. In banishing ourselves from experiencing negativity, we only, paradoxically, make the fact that we do that much worse. The third is what it is – and accepts it.

<u>Third scenario:</u>

1. "You did such a good job out there, I'm proud of you."

2. "It's OK, you'll do better next time, I know it."

Self-compassion: "Hm, that didn't go so well."

The first statement reaffirms that being proud of someone is connected to doing well. Implied is the reverse: that if you don't do a good job, you'll lose that pride. The second statement looks on its surface to be kind, but the subtext is: things will be better... when you get this right. The third statement is just an honest appraisal of the reality of the situation. No rushing in to make excuses or deny what is. No judgment. No implication that your failure is only acceptable if it forms part of a success later on. Just an acknowledgement.

To practice self-compassion in our daily lives, it might emerge that it's the little things that really count. The words you speak, the thoughts you think: these are what make up the texture and tone of your life. As a way to start incorporating more self-compassion into your life, start with the little things first. Beware of judging yourself for doing self-compassion "wrong". If it doesn't feel good to feel good about who you are just yet, that's OK. Choose to feel good about where you are anyway.

Daily Self-compassion: Parenting

For a while, it was popular, in the Western world at least, to help your kids develop a high confidence in themselves. Parents were encouraged never to criticize their children or make them feel second best. As a reaction to perceived pressures in the education system and the increasing competitiveness of colleges, parents understandably wanted to let their children know that they were, in no uncertain terms, valuable. This meant telling them they were perfect and brilliant, and should never settle for anything less.

But the message has become warped over time. Somehow, making sure that your kids didn't suffer a low self esteem it became a project to make sure that their self esteem was *high*. Kids needed to feel special, to have indomitable confidence in themselves and their abilities, no matter what. The irony is that kids raised in this generation are no more secure and happy in themselves as the generations that came before them.

Psychologists are now discovering that over praising children can have the opposite effect. Telling children they're doing better than they are causes them to doubt themselves, even wonder if others are lying to them. A child who thinks they are already high achievers are less likely to take beneficial risks or get a thick enough skin to improve on their competencies. You are in effect setting them up for disappointment in the real world. What's worse, over praising achievements sends out the message: love is conditional.

How to raise children who are self-compassionate:

- Give your child the feeling that your love in them is secure by consistently being there to support – *no matter what.*

- Give your children realistic goals to aim for. Age appropriate tasks that help build competence slowly and steadily teach your child a valuable lesson in hard work.

- Whatever you do, don't compare your child to others, especially not their siblings. Speak about their worth in absolute terms, and not how they compare to their classmates.

- Don't encourage all-or-nothing perfectionism. When your child fails, don't make a big deal of it. Encourage them to keep going.

- Have compassion for yourself – children need good role models to learn how to value themselves.

But, now that we've got the children out the way, we can address the other side of the coin. For many parents, how good a job they're doing raising their children can be a constant source of worry and lack of confidence. Here are some things to help you relax and let go of the pressure to be perfect.

- Remind yourself that everyone will make a mistake here and there, and that it doesn't mean you're doing your children a disservice.

- Resist comparing yourself to other parents. You're different and you're children are different. Comparisons will only make you feel insecure.

- Try to remember that mistakes in life – yours or your child's – can always be teaching moments. Give your child a good understanding of how to be compassionate with *you*.

Daily Self-compassion: Weathering Rejection

Ginny had a really good first date with someone she found she liked a lot. She hadn't found time lately to meet and go out with people, but this guy in particular really stood out for her. But then, after they had made arrangements to meet again later the next week, her date called to cancel. When she tried to organize another meeting a few days later, her messages were met with stone cold silence. It dawned on her slowly and then all at once: she had been rejected.

Here is an imaginary script of Ginny's "inner talk" as she

stewed over the incident for a few weeks.

"I still don't get what happened. We got on SO well. We were laughing, agreeing with one another. There was such a lot of chemistry. He even said himself he couldn't wait to meet again. So what gives? Is there something I don't know? Am I just an idiot who thinks they get on well with people when I really don't? Oh God, maybe he hated every second of the date and was just humoring me all along. Maybe he saw something I didn't. Maybe everyone sees me like that. Maybe I'm really a big loser and haven't figured it out yet. Was it my dress? I knew I shouldn't have worn that. I knew it. Maybe I shouldn't have gone on and on about my holiday to Germany. He was smiling at the time but I bet he was bored to tears. I don't know why I even bother any more. I feel so humiliated. Maybe I'm just not cut out for this dating nonsense, maybe..."

And so on and so on. Ginny's self talk may seem a bit overblown to you, but anyone who's nursed a wound of this kind will know that the negative self talk can get out of hand very quickly. Rejection of this kind can feel like an almost literal slap in the face – someone not only judged you, but they judged you and found you wanting. Here is the kind of inner talk Ginny might have had if she had a more stable self-concept and a little self-compassion after the same incident:

"I still don't get what happened. I thought we got on so well. When I think about it, I didn't say anything hurtful and I definitely wasn't rude... it must be more to do with him. Who knows? I'm feeling pretty fragile about the whole thing but since I can't find anything obviously wrong I'm just going to assume that there's a reason he didn't get in touch. Maybe he's met someone else, or maybe he likes me but realized he isn't really ready to commit to a partner right now. I get that. I mean, I've been there myself. I hate to admit it, but maybe our connection wasn't as strong as I remember. Oh well, it's a pity, but I'm not going to take it personally. I'm going to stop stressing about this now and get on with things. I don't have to be everyone's cup of tea... after all, not everybody is mine..."

A lot of dating experts will deal with Ginny's hurt at being rejected by trying to swing her self esteem the other way: not only does she *not* deserve rejection, but she's better than the date that rejected her. She's fabulous, and if he couldn't see it, then that's his problem etc. The problem with this approach is that these feelings of self-worth are not stable and lasting – when (and not if!) Ginny is rejected again, it will all fall to pieces.

Rejection can be so difficult to deal with because it strikes a blow to our ego, the very thing keeping our sense of pride and self-worth held together. Romantic rejection can be particularly painful, and being found unattractive by the very people we are attracted to can make us feel completely unworthy.

But because the stress of rejection is so heavily tied in with the ego, we can learn to moderate and manage rejection by managing our egos, too. Your ego may be telling you that if you are rejected, it must be because of who you are and what you did, and is proof that you are fundamentally wrong somehow. But think for a minute about the people *you* have rejected in your life – and yes, you have been the rejecter, at times!

You may have turned them down romantically because you just didn't "click" with them, because you were busy (really), a little unsure of yourself or simply not that interested. Maybe, in a rare instance, you felt yourself thinking, "this person is fundamentally wrong somehow", but more than likely, your reasons for the rejection were your own. Understand that people will reject you for a host of reasons, but very seldom because you are unlovable at your core.

Even at it's worst, someone will reject you because, well, they don't like you. On the other hand it's unhealthy to think that everyone will. Part of what makes being human so amazing is how different we all are. Sometimes we connect well with each other, sometimes not. There is no need to dwell on this fact, simply move on to find the people that *do* like you.

Your ego may feel bruised enough that it tries a different approach: that if someone doesn't see and agree with the beauty and perfection that you offer, then it's really their loss, and you're better off without them. As a matter of fact, they did you a favor by removing themselves from your life, and it is you who judges and rejects them. Sound familiar? This is a knee-jerk response to the pain of rejection and completely understandable, however in the long term it only reinforces the same old mechanisms that keep you trapped in a cycle of narcissism and shame, cycling between feeling wonderful and feeling awful.

The trouble with developing such a "thick skin" and sassy attitude is that it could numb you to valuable lessons. Sometimes, although we would rather die than hear it, people's criticisms of us have a kernel of truth, and were we to engage them we'd find that they are not some heartless monsters out to get us. Probably right this minute you can think of at least one person that you feel this way about: no matter what feedback they get from the world, they can't seem to "see" what you do.

In order to grow and become better, we have to admit to

ourselves what isn't working. Be brutally honest with yourself – do you have any blind spots? Are there ways you could improve? But once you've realistically appraised this, the self-compassion can kick in. It's *OK* that you have blind spots and weakness. When we act from a mindful position of self-compassion, we can experience, deeply, the full range of pain at being rejected. We can see, in full clarity, our deficiencies as human beings, and we can mourn it completely. But, we can also know that even *this* pain does not negate our worth as human beings There is no need to hate ourselves or the people who reject us.

The story of the "empty boats":

There is an old Buddhist parable about "empty boats". Imagine you are floating along a river in a boat. All of a sudden, an empty boat comes floating along and bumps into yours. What do you think of this? Probably, you're not angry about it. It's just a boat; it's just something that happened. Now, imagine instead that the boat that knocks into yours is not empty but driven by a person. In this case, you may feel irritated or even angry. Why don't they look where they're going?

The thing is, in both cases, the boats are in a sense empty. The second boat has a person inside, but that person is distracted or thinking of something else. In other words, his bumping into you is not different from an empty boat bumping into you – both have no deliberate consciousness guiding the action.

There is no point getting upset with people who wrong us by being mindless. Getting angry with such a person is like getting angry that an empty boat drifted against yours – it's just a thing that happened. Our modern world is filled with people who are quick to see fault, quick to blame and quick to seek revenge. We devolve into mindless hatred when left alone and anonymous on the Internet, and we are happy to immediately see the worst in other people's actions, to condemn them, to feel indignant.

Save your energy and don't bother reacting to empty boats. In the vast majority of cases, when you feel slighted it's not because someone was deliberately malicious towards you. Rather, we all have moments when our own lives distract us and keep us from considering others as fully as we should. This is unfortunate, but there is no point in getting angry about it.

When you feel offended, stop to ask yourself whether you might be taking it too personally. Be compassionate with people who hurt you by accident and without thinking. After all, you have almost certainly done the same to others.

Chapter Six: Forgiveness, Boundaries and Assertiveness

How did the previous story make you feel?

For many people, forgiveness of others' transgressions is a near impossibility. They may feel angry and insulted even reading about it. What kind of a pushover would they be if they simply let everyone's boat bash into theirs all the time?

Assertiveness that stems from the ego

When a child is bullied at school and their parents tell them that the correct response is to fight back, they are sending the message that the way to reinforce personal boundaries is with violence. Even if our parents were more conciliatory, many adults grow up with the idea that to put up a boundary and have people respect it is a process filled with conflict. When someone oversteps the mark, we are encouraged to act from our anger and retaliate. Sadly, our actions to defend ourselves start to look very much like the actions we hate experiencing ourselves.

Assertiveness from compassion

While nobody would argue that it's vital to have a healthy sense of your own boundaries, it's not necessarily healthy to act out from anger. It isn't helpful to get angry and annihilate the boat that drifted into yours. Smashing the boat to bits in a fit of indignation is not necessary, nor do you have to get the boat to admit its fault and apologize. It's just something that happened. Move the boat out of the way and get on with it.

For those unused to it, compassion may seem incompatible with assertiveness. Having kindness for others seems like an achievable goal, but what about when people abuse that kindness? What about those people that actually deliberately hurt us?

When we have compassion, we realize that every person has feelings, and if they've done something to hurt another person, chances are strong that they feel remorseful. When we are consumed with resentment and bitterness towards somebody, it can difficult to see that they are also struggling in life, trying in the way they know how to be the best they can – just like you.

We can never go back into the past and make it different from what it is. Simply by being alive, we're signed up for a degree of hurt and disappointment in life. It's just part of being human. Remember back to a time when you hurt someone. If you've been lucky enough to have experienced forgiveness yourself, remember how important it was to you at the time.

If you cannot summon up forgiveness for people who have wronged you right now, then try to do it for yourself. Have you ever looked back at your past and wished you had more grudges, more anger towards others? Let it go. We're all doing the best we can, and sometimes, it falls horribly short and we hurt one another. Forgive anyway and move on.

And you needn't be a pushover. Do not tolerate continued mistreatment from others because you have compassion for yourself, but do not mistreat them in turn because you have compassion for *them*. Learning how to set up and defend a boundary with love and kindness in your heart can be a revelation for those who have suffered abuse, resentment or bitterness in their past.

What would happen now, if you just let it go forever?

Healing grudges, forgiving and moving forward

Look deeply into the pain and anger you feel at someone else. Experience it. Don't push it away and don't chastise yourself for the feelings you have, however ugly. Next, ask what they can teach you. Have you allowed behavior that you shouldn't have? What do you know about yourself now that this pain has taught you? Transform your anger and hostility into defending your boundaries. Anger can mobilize and strengthen you.

But after that, let the anger go. Anger is a potent reminder of the importance of assertive boundaries, but over and above that, it only hurts the one who holds onto it. Read through any agony and advice column and you'll see that the bulk of problems people have could be solved by saying, "I love you but I won't tolerate that". And meaning it.

Conclusion

To enjoy the benefits of mindful self-compassion, we merely need to change our focus. Loving ourselves and being gentle and accepting of the reality of who we are doesn't require any special equipment, knowledge or training. It merely requires that you open your heart and mind, to yourself and to others.

At times, it can feel so easy to succumb to the hatred, impatience and judgment around us. By learning self-compassion, however, we realize the source of this negativity, and become less affected by it. When we embrace the imperfection of being human, we can be resilient enough to face criticism and rejection with grace. By developing and drawing on a deeper well of self-worth, we become immune to self-doubt, low self-confidence, blame, resentment and judgment.

In the West, the concepts of Buddhism are gradually being incorporated into all areas of our lives and appreciated for the peace and tranquility they can bring. In meditating, we learn to let thoughts come and go, and to withhold our judgment of them. Extending this, we can take our practice to include other people. People are not good or bad, and neither are we. In fact, we are all so much more than that – we are all human beings, and truly embracing that can be the start of something profound.

Finally, I would love to hear how this book has helped you. So if you've benefited from it, I would love it if you'd leave a review and tell me all about it. You can leave a review by searching for this title on www.amazon.com

Also, below you will find a bonus preview of my book on stress and how to stop worrying, called "How To Stop Worrying And Start Living – What Other People Think Of Me Is None Of My Business".

Bonus: Preview: "How To Stop Worrying and Start Living - What Other People Think Of Me Is None Of My Business"

Stress is a lot like love – hard to define, but you know it when you feel it.

This book will explore the nature of stress and how it infiltrates every level of your life, including the physical, emotional, cognitive, relational and even spiritual. You'll find ways to nurture resilience, rationality and relaxation in your every day life, and learn how to loosen the grip of worry and anxiety. Through techniques that get to the heart of your unique stress response, and an exploration of how stress can affect your relationships, you'll discover how to control stress instead of letting it control you. This book shows you how.

This book is not just another "anti-stress" book. Here, we will not be concerned with only reducing the symptoms of stress. Rather, we'll try to understand exactly what stress is and the role it plays in our lives. We'll attempt to dig deep to really understand the real sources of our anxiety and how to take ownership of them. Using the power of habit and several techniques for smoothing out the stressful wrinkles in our day-to-day lives, we'll move towards a real-world solution to living with less stress, more confidence and a deep spiritual resilience that will insulate you from the inevitable pressures of life.

We will address physical, emotional, relational, spiritual, and cognitive and behavioral symptoms of stress.

This book will be a little different from most stress-management tools on the market today. While most stress solutions offer relief for symptoms in only one or two of the above areas, this book will show you how all five areas are important, and a successful stress solution will touch on each of them.

By adopting a trusting, open and relaxed attitude, we'll bring something more of ourselves to relationships of all kinds. This book will take a look at dating and relationships without stress and worry, as well as ways to bring tranquility and balance into your home and family life. Again, this book is not about eradicating stress from your life forever. We'll end with a consideration of the positive side of negative thinking, and how we can use stress and worry to our advantage.

Stress has become so commonplace in our modern world that we are actually suspicious of people who claim not to be busy. Our lives keep filling up with more: more events, more responsibilities, more things, more people, more work. Like a bewildered rat in its wheel, we decide there's only one thing to do: keep going.

The consequences may not be obvious immediately, but the effects of stress, anxiety and worry are far-reaching. Wear and tear from stress can include heart disease, increased risk of cancer and even early death. Stress makes you feel awful, obviously, but it's far more serious than that. A stressed out body and mind are simply not everything they could be. Being overwhelmed cognitively means you are never really 100% available to make the best decisions for yourself. You're slower, get tired more quickly, and your memory suffers.

When you're constantly juggling feelings of stress, you're not emotionally available either. You're more prone to depression and pessimism, more likely to abandon projects you start and more likely to interpret things around you in a negative light. Stress also seeps into your relationships. The last thing you want to do is seek out others and be social, and this together with an irritable mood and short temper mean your closest connections become undermined.

You don't necessarily have to be a rushed-off-her-feet working mother or a CEO who's married to his high pressure job to understand how damaging stress can be to your relationships.

For those of us with social anxiety, shyness or difficulties with dating, relationships with others are actually the cause of the stress. Low self esteem, paranoia about the judgment of others, inability to reach out to the opposite sex... Even when you manage to find someone, jealousy and insecurity sabotage your ability to relax and enjoy it. These are all just different manifestations of this strange frame of mind we call "stress".

Stress gets into your body, heart, mind and soul. Stress damages your ability to have trusting, open relationships with others. Saddest of all, stress weakens your relationship with yourself in the form of self doubt, low self confidence and bitterness. We tend to think of stress as nothing more serious than a certain tightness in the shoulders or a schedule that could be a little leaner. But stress can permeate every single area of our lives, right from the presence of stress hormones in the body's tissues to our bigger, overarching sense of who we are as human beings in this world.

This book is for those of us pacing in our cages, tossing at night with heads full of doom and gloom, unable to trust those around us and the world at large.

Other Books By This Author

- Minimalism: How To Declutter, De-Stress And Simplify Your Life With Simple Living

- The Minimalist Budget: A Practical Guide On How To Save Money, Spend Less And Live More With A Minimalist Lifestyle

- How To Stop Worrying and Start Living – What Other People Think Of Me Is None Of My Business: Learn Stress Management and How To Overcome Relationship Jealousy, Social Anxiety and Stop Being Insecure

- Mindful Eating: A Healthy, Balanced and Compassionate Way To Stop Overeating, How To Lose Weight and Get a Real Taste of Life by Eating Mindfully

- Self-Esteem For Kids - Every Parent's Greatest Gift: How To Raise Kids To Have Confidence In Themselves And Their Own Abilities

Bibliography and Further Reading

These are some of the materials that have inspired the ideas in this book. If you have found any value in what has been written here and you'd like to read further on these topics, below are some books, websites and journal articles that might interest you.

"I Hate You Don't Leave Me" by Jerold, Kreisman and Strauss – an excellent book on the psychological condition called Borderline Personality Disorder. Having a self concept that heavily depends on others and a history of tumultuous relationships characterizes this disorder. Even if you don't suffer from BPD, most of us can recognize some of these traits in ourselves. A fascinating read for those with low self esteem that is exacerbated in abusive or unhealthy relationships. http://www.amazon.com/Hate-You-Dont-Leave-Me/dp/0380713055

Tiny Buddha Blog – More than the regular ego-based self help, this blog is a goldmine for wisdom you can actually use in your life. Looking at the inevitable challenges of living through the lens of Eastern philosophy, this blog is written from the heart and it shows.
Www.tinybuddha.com

A fantastic website with ample links to other resources. Watch the short video on the front page for an inspirational discussion of how self-compassion compares to ego-based self esteem.

Www.selfcompassion.org

"The Courage to Heal" by Ellen Bass is a great book tackling questions of forgiveness, resentment and healing wounds from our past, specifically childhood sexual abuse. If you have a history of abuse as a child or have experienced betrayal by others, this may be a very healing book for you.

http://www.amazon.com/Courage-Heal-Survivors-Sexual-Anniversary/dp/0061284335/ref=sr_1_1?s=books&ie=UTF8&qid=1408008108&sr=1-1&keywords=survivors+of+child+abuse

"Why do I do that?" by Dr. Joseph Burgo - Simply one of the best books out there on the link between shame and narcissism. If you have identified issues with either narcissism or very low self esteem (i.e., shame), and you would like a deeper, more psychoanalytic exploration of how the two are connected, this book will be eye-opening.

http://www.amazon.com/Why-Do-That-Psychological-Mechanisms/dp/0988443120/ref=sr_1_1?s=books&ie=UTF8&qid=1408008226&sr=1-1&keywords=why+do+I+do+that%3F

Also see Dr. Burgo's blog, where he addresses issues of narcissism, shame and self esteem in different posts. www.afterpsychotherapy.com

An interesting article on emotional abuse http://www.counselingcenter.illinois.edu/self-help-brochures/relationship-problems/emotional-abuse/

Plenty of resources on the topic of self-compassionate www.mindfulselfcompassion.org

Interesting articles about Wabi Sabi http://c2.com/cgi/wiki?WabiSabi

A great resource for compassionate parenting and more http://www.nonviolentcommunication.com/parenting_tips/

Compassion, dating and rejection – a great site and great article http://www.baggagereclaim.co.uk/give-yourself-the-gift-of-self-compassion-stop-judging-you-the-rejection-will-subside/

A brilliant book by Brene Brown, who writes and speaks about shame, authenticity and happiness http://www.amazon.com/Gifts-Imperfection-Think-

Supposed-

Embrace/dp/159285849X/ref=sr_1_3?s=books&ie=UTF8&qi
d=1408008641&sr=1-3&keywords=self+esteem

---

i   "The blame game: the effect of responsibility and social
stigma on empathy for pain."
http://www.ncbi.nlm.nih.gov/pubmed/19425830
ii   "Practising compassion increases happiness and self esteem"
http://link.springer.com/article/10.1007%2Fs10902-010-9239-1
iii   "An fMRI study of caring vs self-focus during induced
compassion and pride"
        http://www.ncbi.nlm.nih.gov/pubmed/21896494
iv   Compassion Meditation Study
        http://tibet.emory.edu/cbct/research.html
v   "Changing Relationship Growth Belief: Intrapersonal and
Interpersonal Consequences of Compassionate Goals."
        http://www.ncbi.nlm.nih.gov/pubmed/21949478
vi   "Upward spirals of the heart: autonomic flexibility, as
indexed by vagal tone, reciprocally and prospectively predicts
positive emotions and social connectedness."
        http://www.ncbi.nlm.nih.gov/pubmed/20851735

9197128R00041

Printed in Great Britain
by Amazon.co.uk, Ltd.,
Marston Gate.